EASY PIANO

ONE DIRECTION MADE IN THE A.M.

T0077023

ISBN 978-1-4950-5756-4

HAL•LEONARD®
CORPORATION

7777 W. BLUEMOUND RD. P.O. BOX 13819 MILWAUKEE, WI 53213

Visit Hal Leonard Online at
www.halleonard.com

HEY ANGEL

Words and Music by JOHN HENRY RYAN,
JULIAN BUNETTA and EDWARD DREWETT

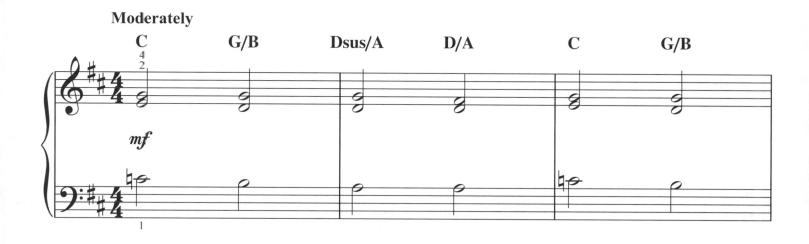

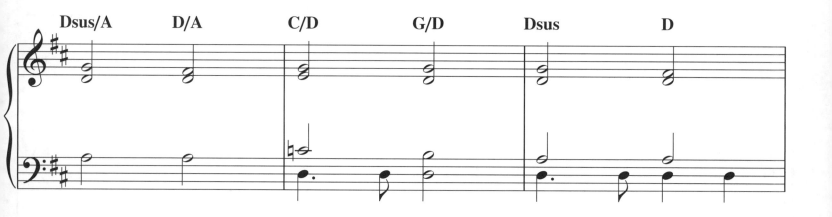

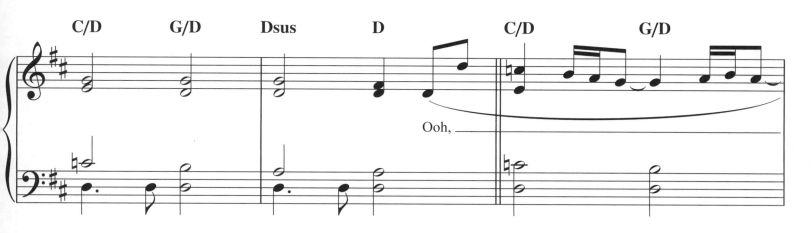

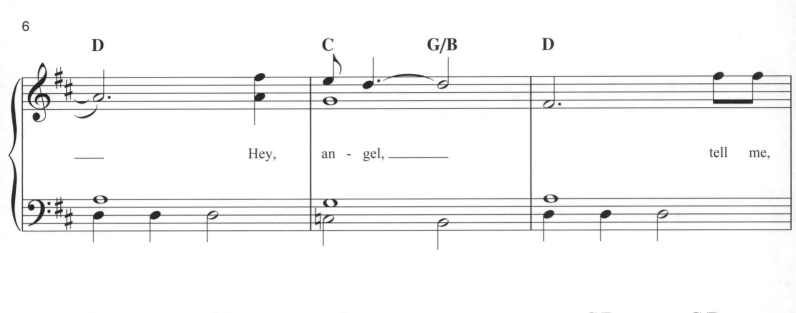

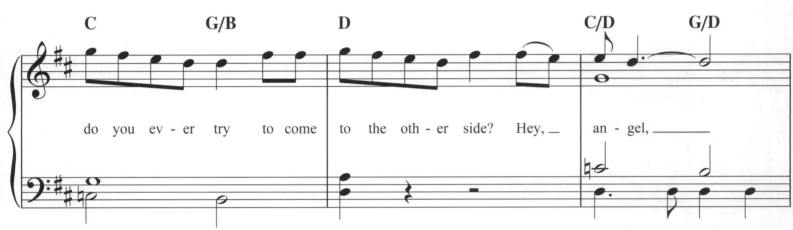

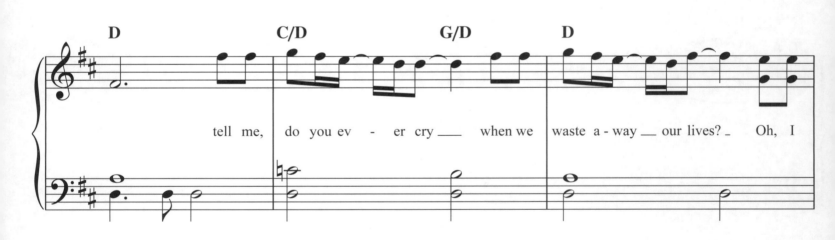

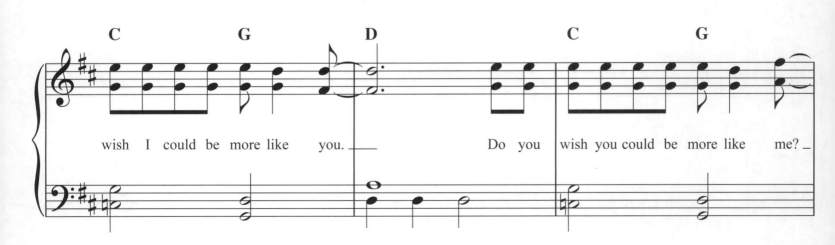

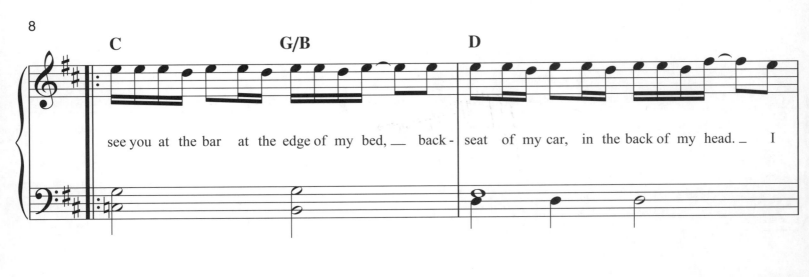

see you at the bar at the edge of my bed, __ back-seat of my car, in the back of my head. __ I

1.

come a-live when I hear your voice. __ It's a beau-ti-ful sound, it's a beau-ti-ful noise. I

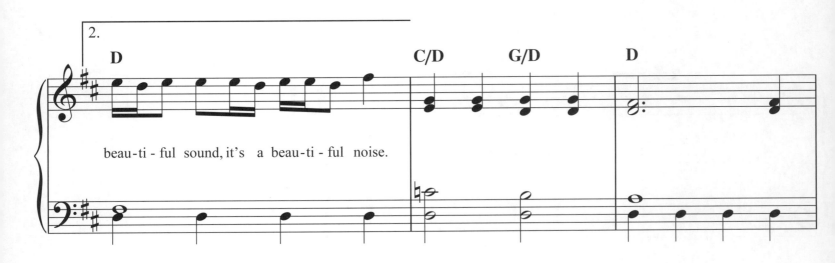

2.

beau-ti-ful sound, it's a beau-ti-ful noise.

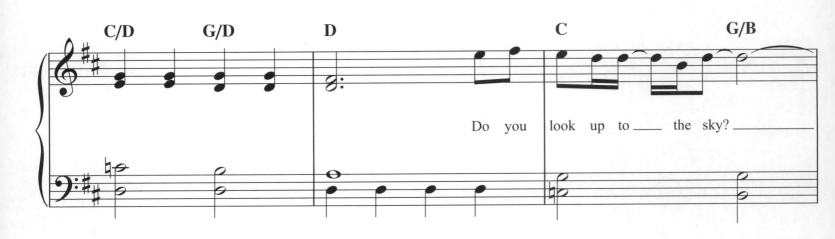

Do you look up to __ the sky? __

Do you look up to ____ the sky? ____ Oh, I

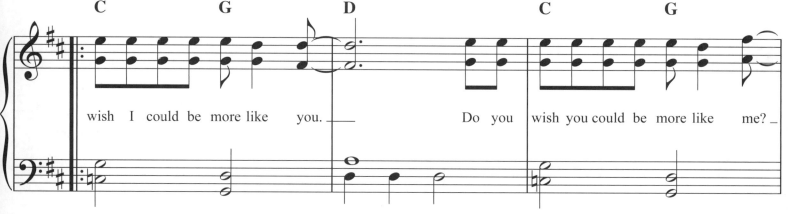

wish I could be more like you. ____ Do you wish you could be more like me? _

1. Oh, I ____ 2. Hey, an - gel, ____

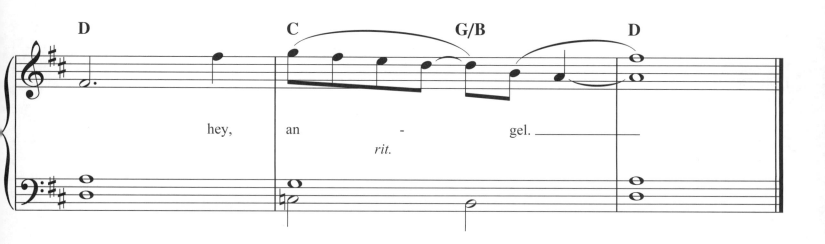

hey, an - gel. ____

rit.

DRAG ME DOWN

Words and Music by JOHN HENRY RYAN,
JAMIE SCOTT and JULIAN BUNETTA

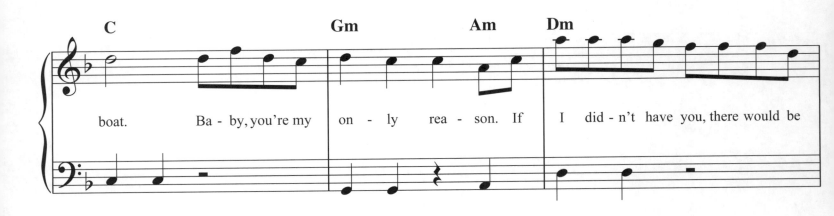

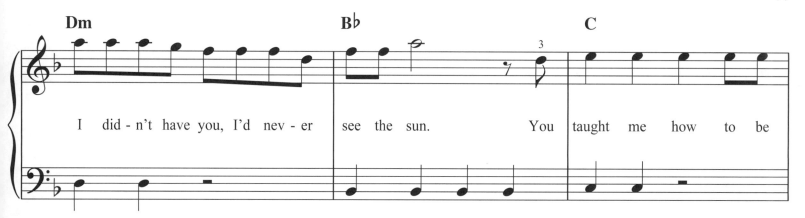

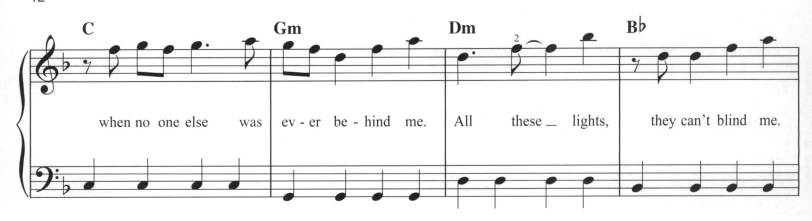

when no one else was ev - er be - hind me. All these __ lights, they can't blind me.

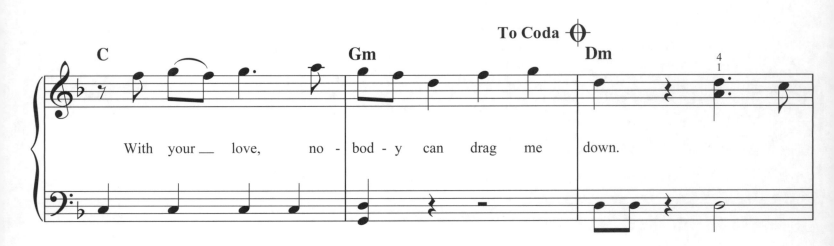

With your __ love, no - bod - y can drag me down.

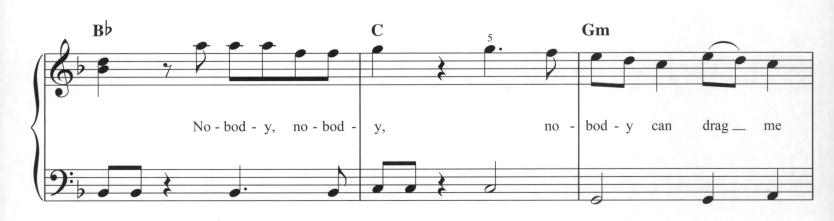

No - bod - y, no - bod - y, no - bod - y can drag __ me

down. __ No - bod - y, no - bod - y, no -

PERFECT

Words and Music by HARRY STYLES,
LOUIS TOMLINSON, JOHN HENRY RYAN,
JESSE SHATKIN, MAUREEN McDONALD,
JACOB HINDLIN and JULIAN BUNETTA

Moderately

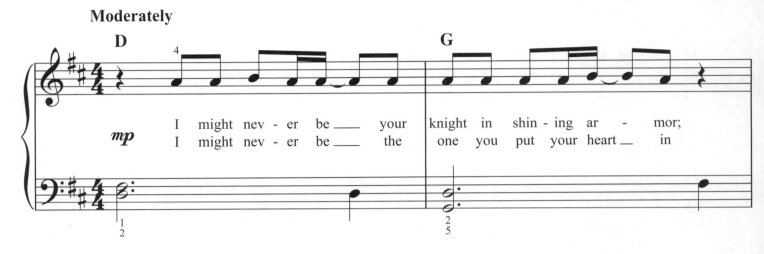

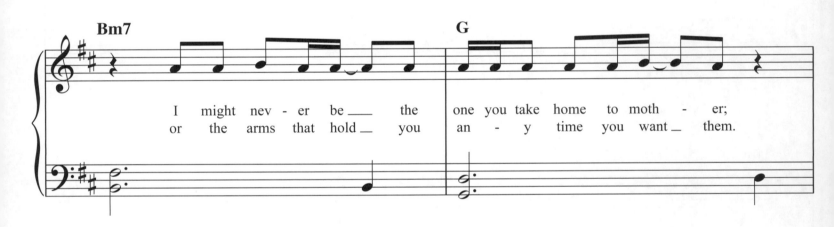

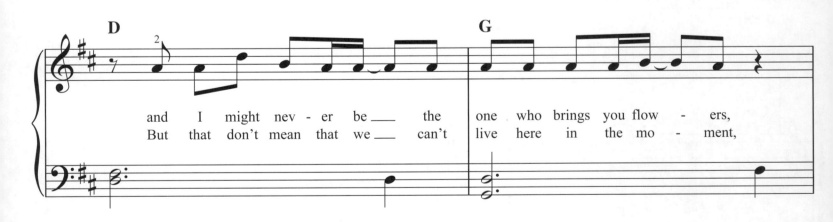

but I can be the one, ___ be the one to-night.
'cause I can be the one you love from time to time.

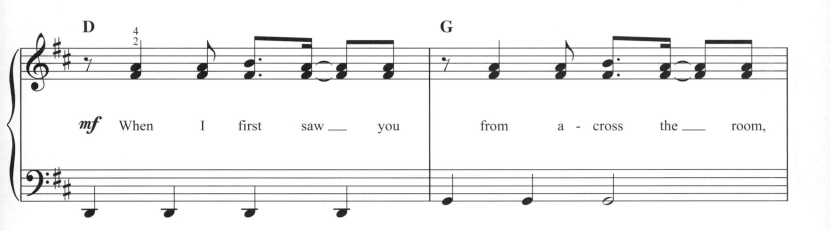

mf When I first saw ___ you from a-cross the ___ room,

I could tell that you were cu-ri-ous, oh yeah. ___

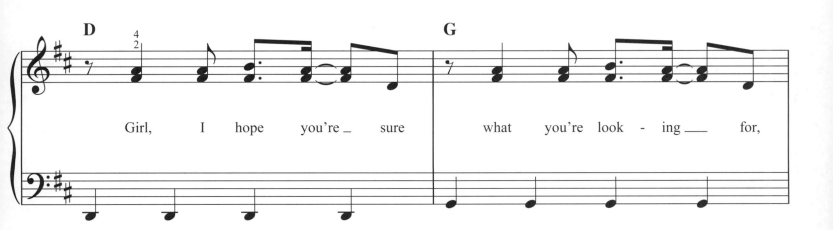

Girl, I hope you're ___ sure what you're look-ing ___ for,

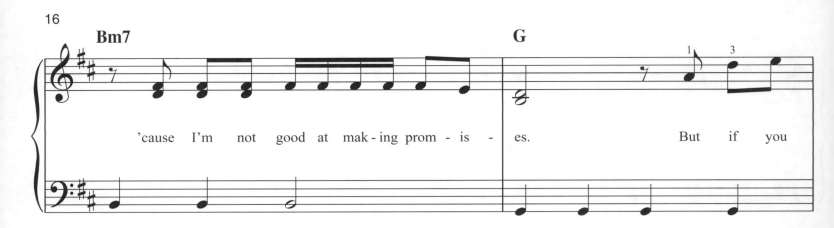

'cause I'm not good at mak-ing prom-is - es. But if you

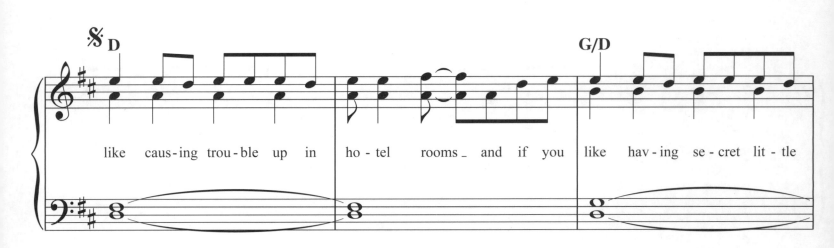

like caus-ing trou-ble up in ho-tel rooms _ and if you like hav-ing se-cret lit-tle

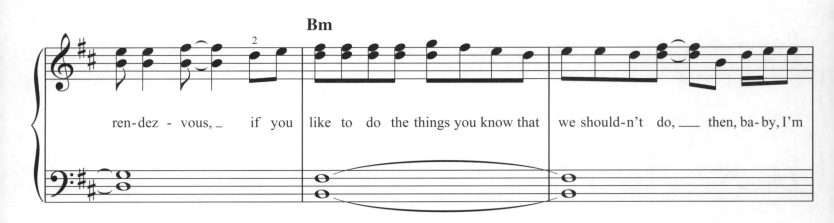

ren-dez - vous, _ if you like to do the things you know that we should-n't do, _ then, ba-by, I'm

per - fect. _ Ba-by, I'm per - fect for you. _ And if you like mid-night driv-ing with the

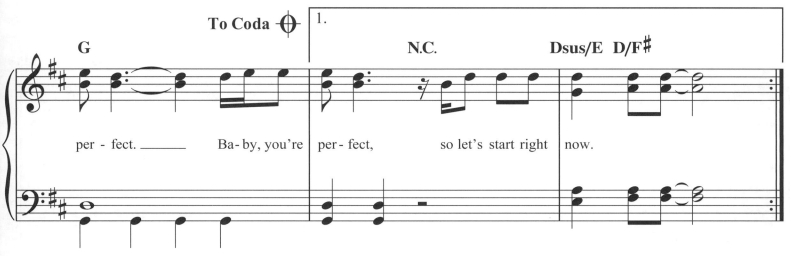

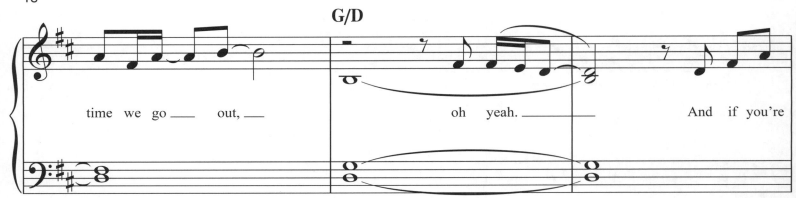

time we go ____ out, ____   oh yeah. _____   And if you're

look-ing for some-one to write your   break-up songs a-bout, ___ ba-by, I'm

per-fect. _____ Ba-by, we're   per-fect. _____ If you

CODA

per-fect,   so let's start right now.

INFINITY

Words and Music by JOHN HENRY RYAN,
JULIAN BUNETTA and JAMIE SCOTT

Half-time Ballad

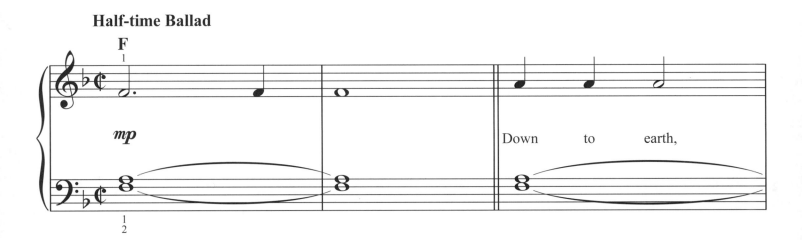

Down to earth,

keep on fall-ing when I know __ it hurts. Go-ing fast-er than a

mil - lion miles an hour, try'n' to catch my breath some way, some -

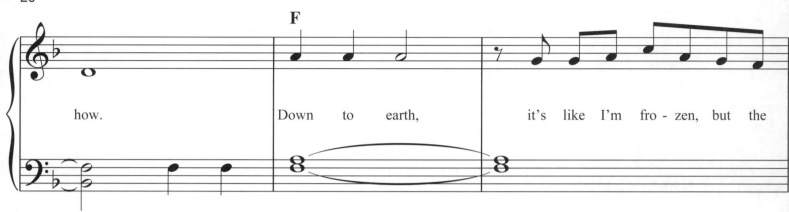

how.

Down to earth,

it's like I'm fro - zen, but the

world still turns.

Stuck in mo - tion, but the

wheels __ keep spin - ning

'round,

mov - ing in re - verse with no way

out.

And now

I'm one ____ step

clos - er to ____ be - ing

two ____ steps

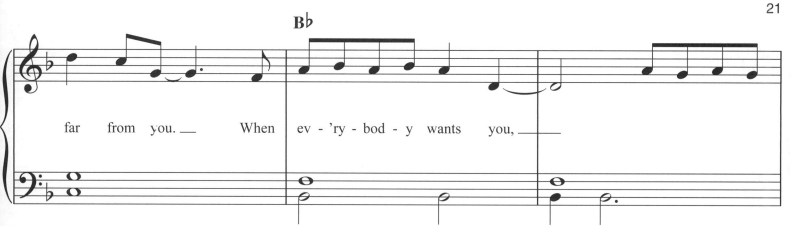

far from you. ___ When ev - 'ry - bod - y wants you, ___

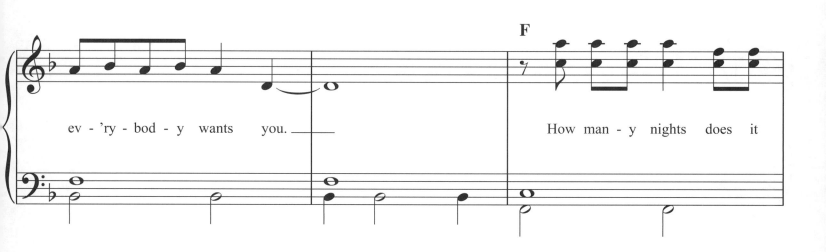

ev - 'ry - bod - y wants you. ___ How man - y nights does it

take to count ___ the stars? That's the time it would take to fix ___ my

heart. Oh, ba - by, I was there ___ for you, ___ all I ev - er want - ed was ___ the

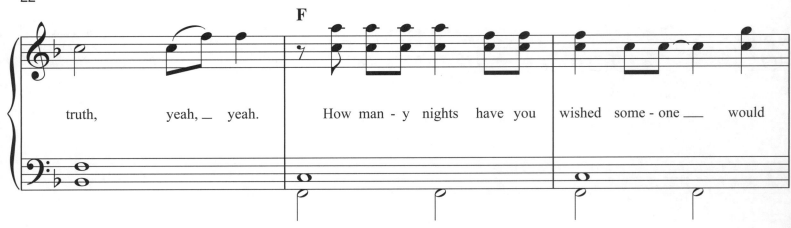

truth, yeah, __ yeah. How man - y nights have you wished some - one __ would

stay? Lie a - wake, on - ly hop - ing they're __ o - kay. I nev - er count - ed

all __ of mine, __ if I tried I know it would feel like in - fin - i - ty.

In - fin - i - ty. __ In - fin - i - ty. __

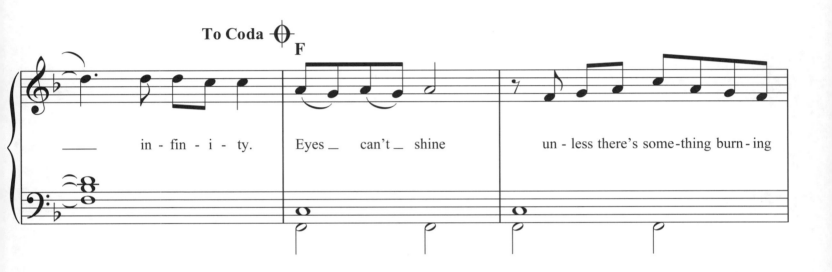

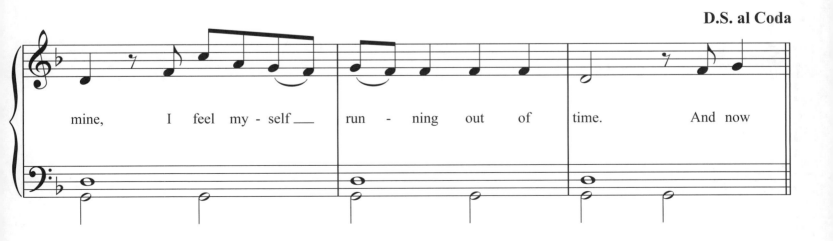

CODA

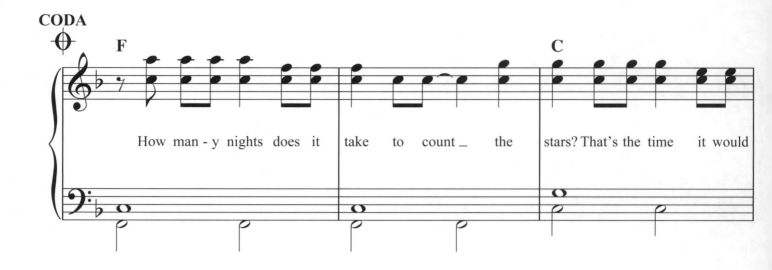

How man-y nights does it take to count __ the stars? That's the time it would

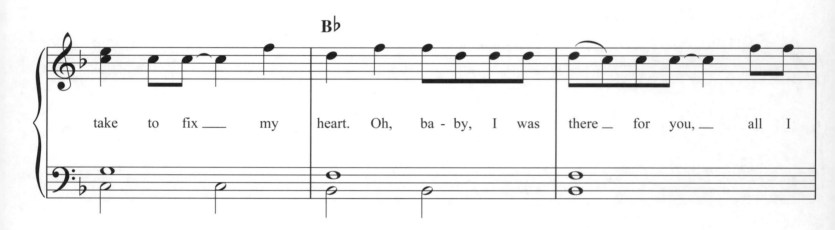

take to fix __ my heart. Oh, ba-by, I was there __ for you, __ all I

ev-er want-ed was __ the truth, yeah, __ yeah. How man-y nights have you

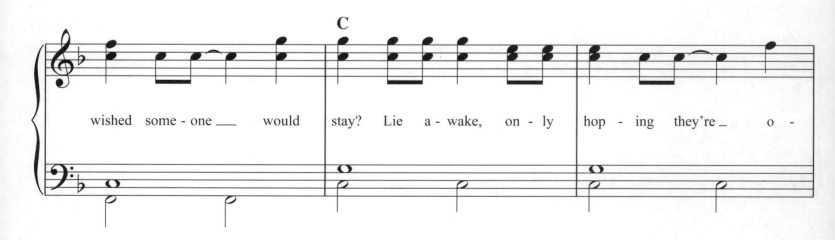

wished some-one __ would stay? Lie a-wake, on-ly hop-ing they're __ o-

END OF THE DAY

Words and Music by LIAM PAYNE, LOUIS TOMLINSON,
JOHN HENRY RYAN, WAYNE ANTHONY HECTOR,
JULIAN BUNETTA, EDWARD DREWETT,
GAMAL LEWIS and JACOB HINDLIN

Pop Rock

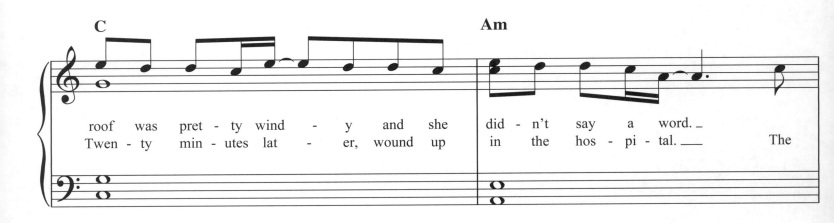

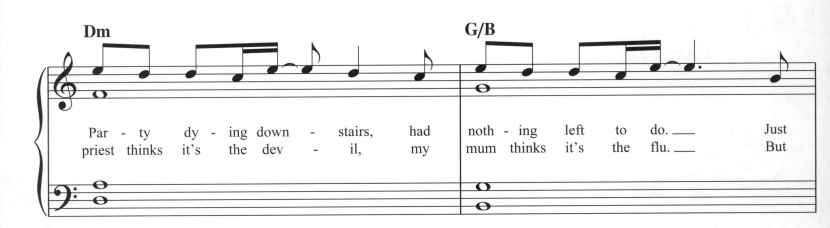

me,   her and   the moon. I said, "You're __ on

girl, it's on - ly you.

fire, babe," __   then down came __ the light - ning ___ on me. __

**Suddenly much slower,
moderate Ballad**

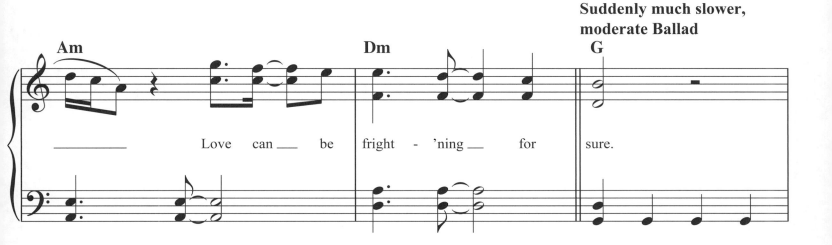

_____ Love can __ be fright - 'ning __ for sure.

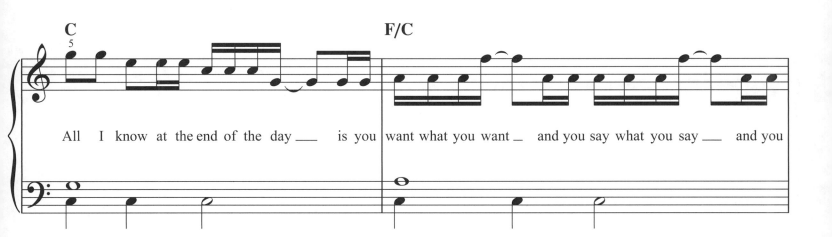

All I know at the end of the day ___ is you want what you want __ and you say what you say ___ and you

G/C   Dm   C/E   F   G

fol - low your heart __ e - ven though it - 'll break __ some - times. __

C   F/C

All   I   know at the end of the day __ is you love who you love, __ there ain't no oth-er way. __ If there's

To Coda ⊕

G/C   Dm7   C/E   F   G

some-thing I've learned __ from a mil-lion mis-takes; __ you're the one that I want __ at the end of the day. __

C   F/C

Oh. __   Oh. __   Oh. __

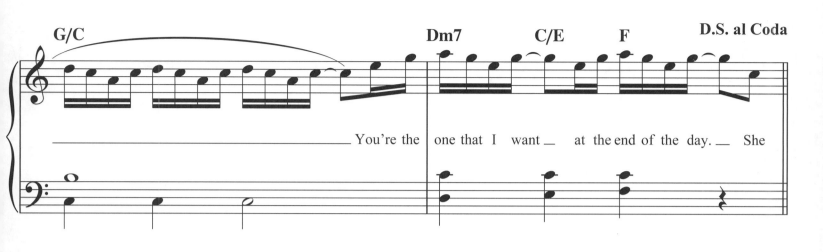

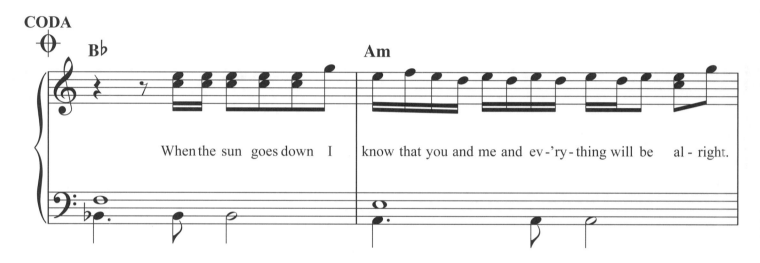

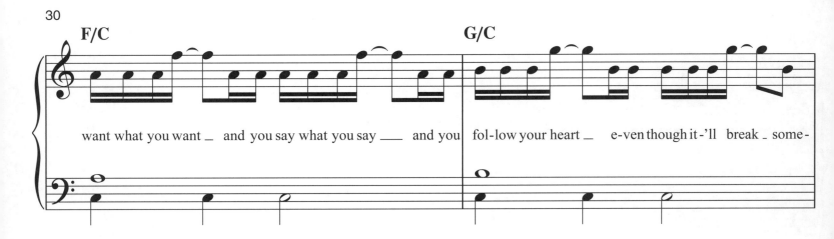

F/C   **G/C**

want what you want _ and you say what you say ___ and you fol-low your heart _ e-ven though it-'ll break _ some-

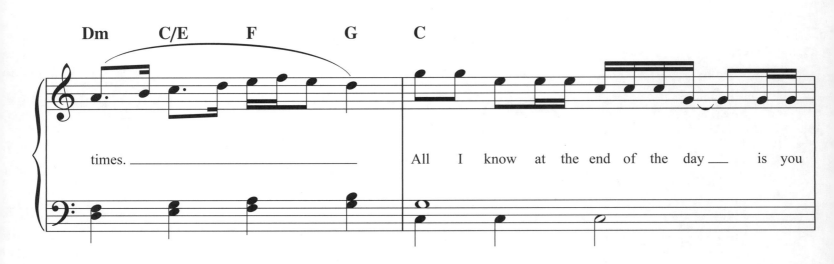

Dm   **C/E**   **F**   **G**   **C**

times. _____   All   I   know   at the end of the day __   is you

F/C

love   who   you   love, ___   there   ain't   no   oth - er   way. ___   If   there's

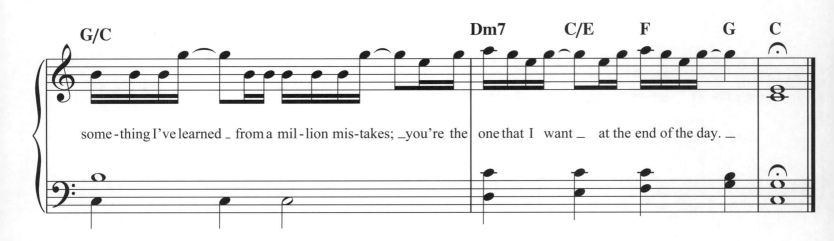

G/C   **Dm7**   **C/E**   **F**   **G**   **C**

some-thing I've learned _ from a mil-lion mis-takes; _you're the one that I want _ at the end of the day. _

IF I COULD FLY

Words and Music by HARRY STYLES,
JOHAN CARLSSON and ROSS GOLAN

32

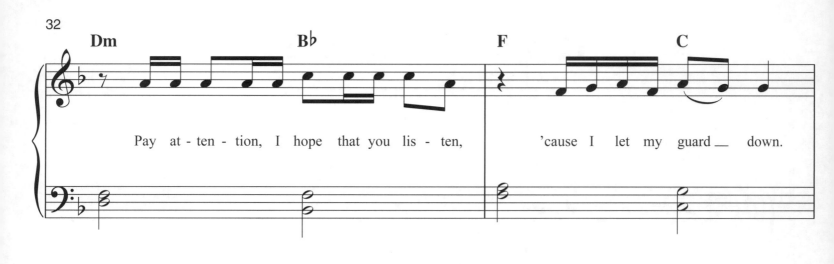

Pay at-ten-tion, I hope that you lis-ten, 'cause I let my guard down.

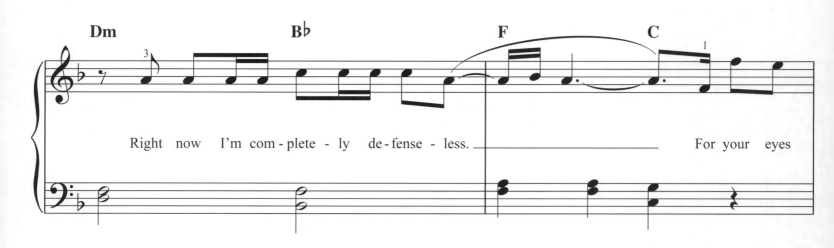

Right now I'm com-plete-ly de-fense-less. For your eyes

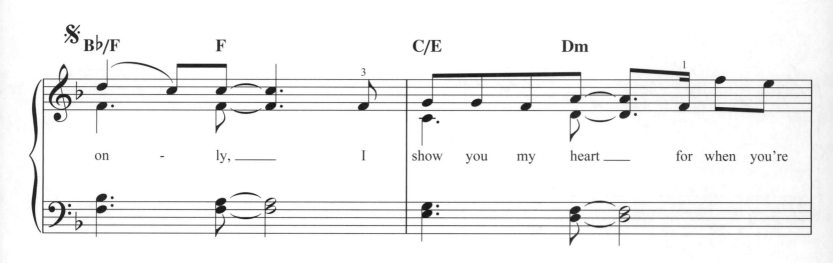

on-ly, I show you my heart for when you're

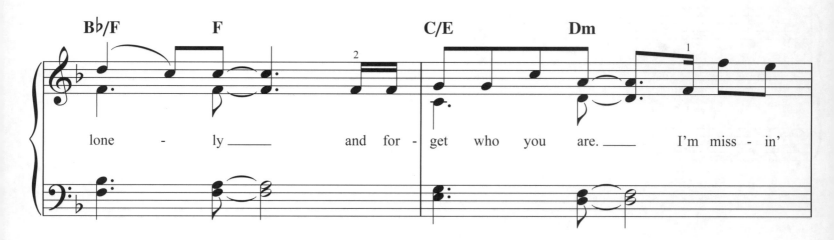

lone-ly and for-get who you are. I'm miss-in'

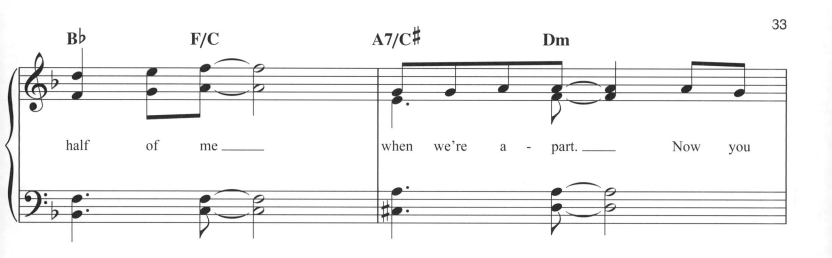

Bb　　　**F/C**　　　　　**A7/C#**　　　　**Dm**

half　of　me　　　　when we're a - part.　　Now you

Bb　　**F/A**　　　　**Bb**　　**F/A**　　　**Bb**　　**F/A**　　　　　**To Coda** ⊕

know　me,　　for your eyes　　on - ly,　　　　　for your eyes

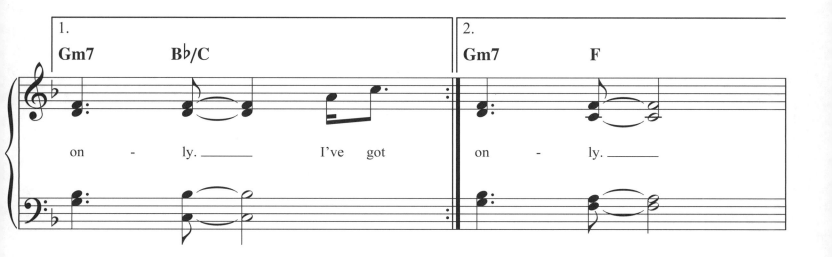

1.
Gm7　　　**Bb/C**

on　-　ly.　　　　I've　got

2.
Gm7　　　　**F**

on　-　ly.

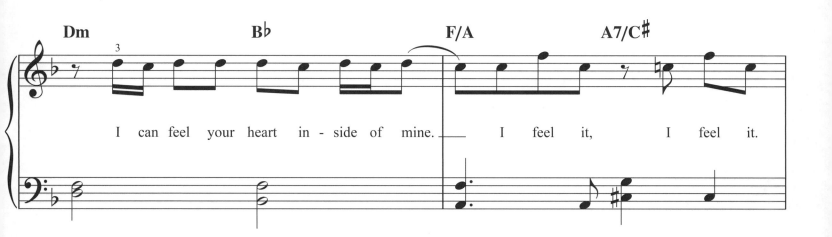

Dm　　　　　　　　　　**Bb**　　　　　　**F/A**　　　　**A7/C#**

I can feel your heart in - side of mine.　　I feel it,　I feel it.

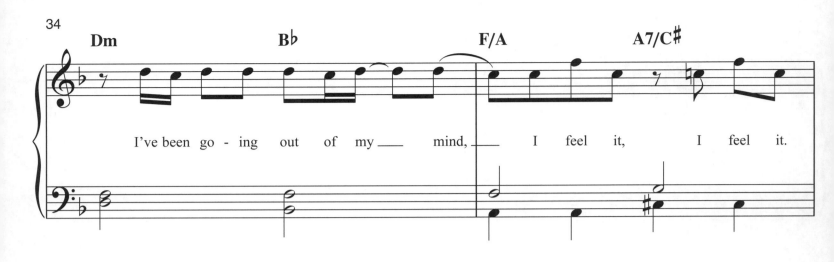

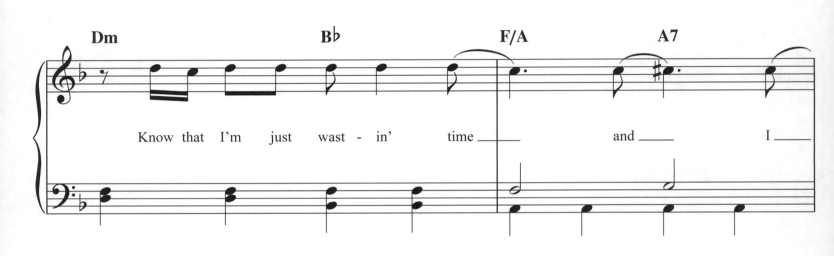

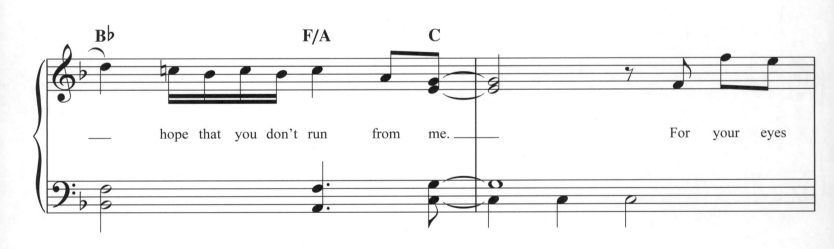

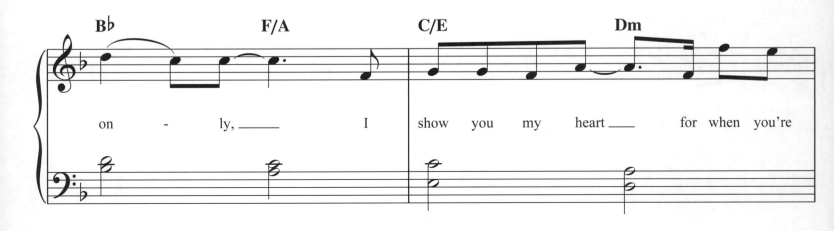

lone - ly _____ and for - get who you are. _____ I'm miss - in'

half of me _____ when we're a - part. _____ Now you

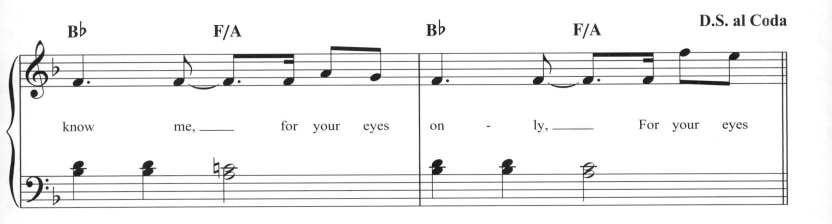

D.S. al Coda

know me, _____ for your eyes on - ly, _____ For your eyes

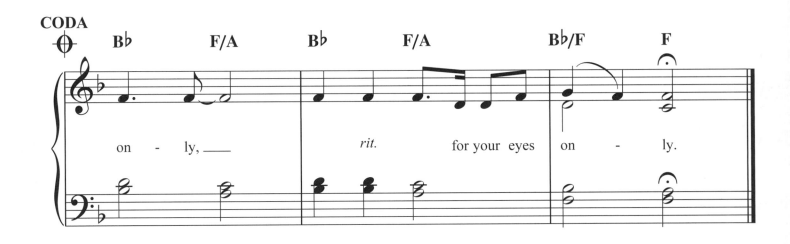

CODA

on - ly, _____ *rit.* for your eyes on - ly.

LONG WAY DOWN

Words and Music by LIAM PAYNE,
LOUIS TOMLINSON, JOHN HENRY RYAN,
JULIAN BUNETTA and JAMIE SCOTT

Moderately

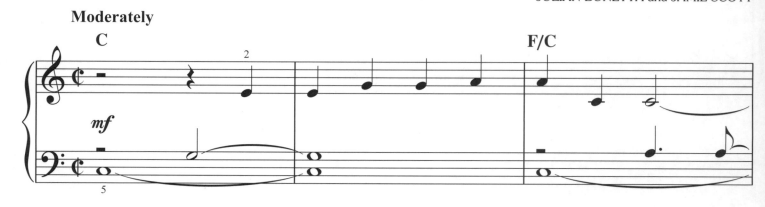

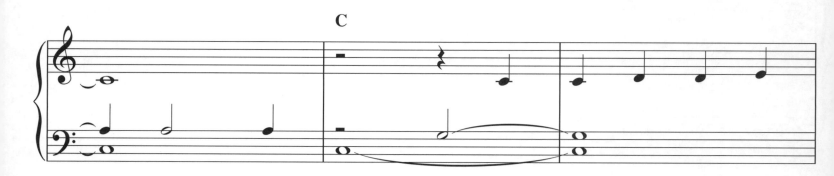

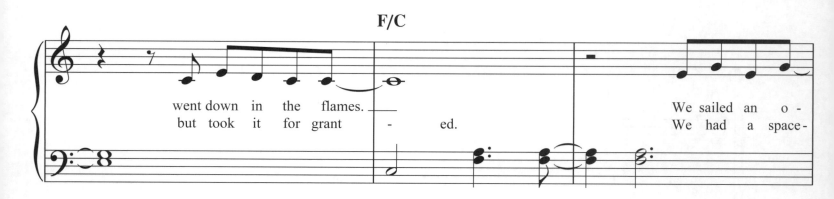

We made a fire. ___ -tain,

went down in the flames. ___
but took it for grant - ed.

We sailed an o -
We had a space -

- cean
- ship,

and drowned in a wave.
but we could-n't land it.

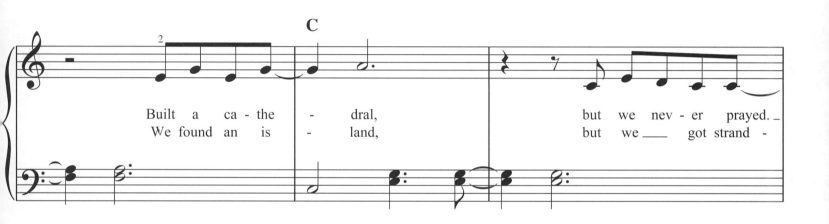

Built a ca - the - dral,
We found an is - land,

but we nev - er prayed.
but we ___ got strand -

- ed.

We did it all, ___ yeah,
We had it all, ___ yeah.

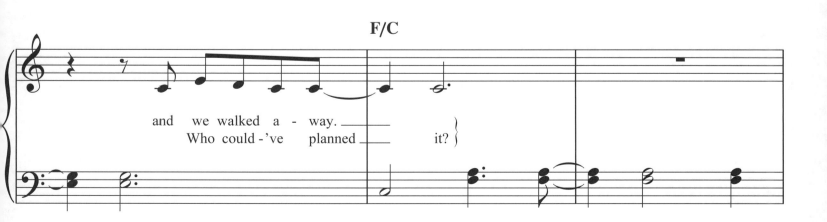

and we walked a - way. ___
Who could -'ve planned ___ it?

Point of no re - turn and now it's just too late to

turn a - round. _____

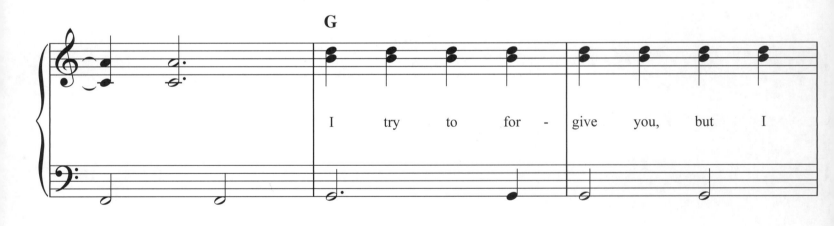

I try to for - give you, but I

strug - gle 'cause I don't know how. _____

We built it up so

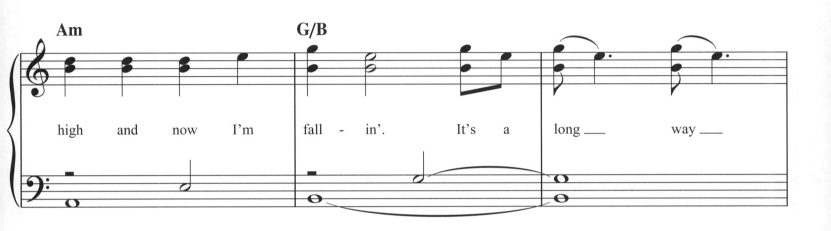

high and now I'm fall - in'. It's a long ___ way ___

down. ___ It's a

To Coda ⊕

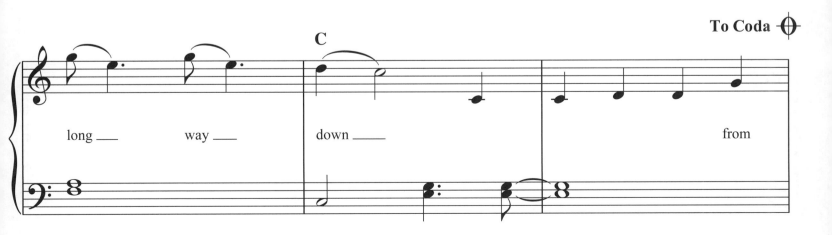

long ___ way ___ down ___ from

D.S. al Coda

CODA

here.   We had a moun-

here,

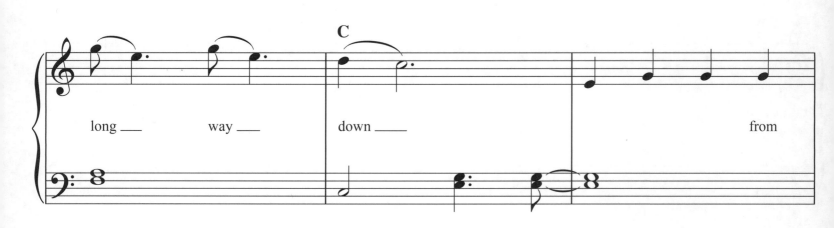

long   way   down   from

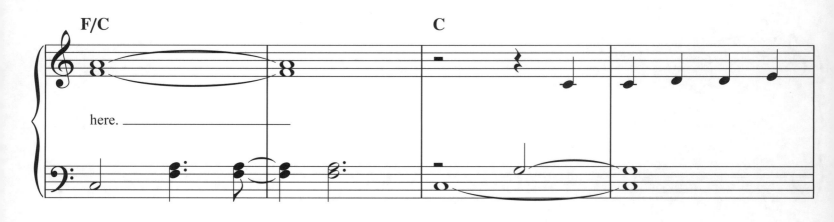

here.

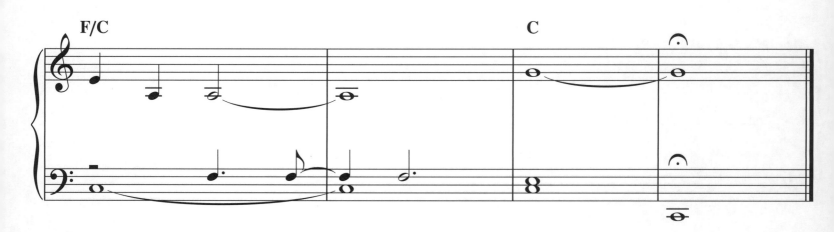

OLIVIA

Words and Music by HARRY STYLES,
JOHN HENRY RYAN and JULIAN BUNETTA

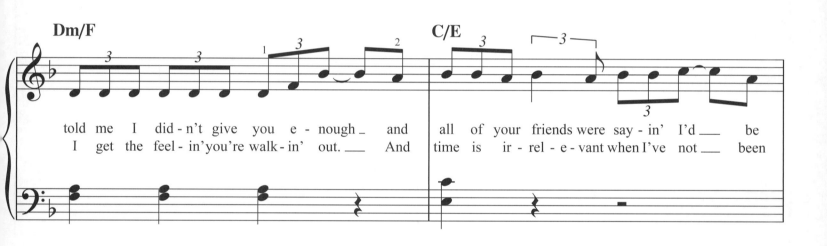

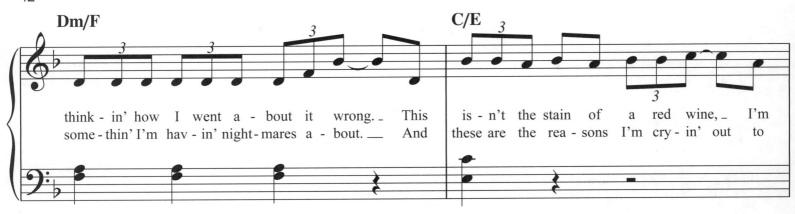

Dm/F ... **C/E**

think - in' how I went a - bout it wrong. __ This is - n't the stain of a red wine, __ I'm
some - thin' I'm hav - in' night - mares a - bout. __ And these are the rea - sons I'm cry - in' out to

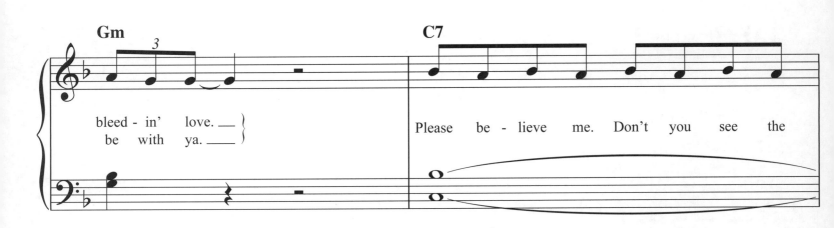

Gm ... **C7**

bleed - in' love. __
be with ya. __

Please be - lieve me. Don't you see the

Gm7

things you mean to me? Oh, I love you, I love you, I love - a, love - a, love O -

liv - i - a. I live for you, I long for you, O -

liv - i - a. I've been i - dol - iz - in' the light in your eyes, O -

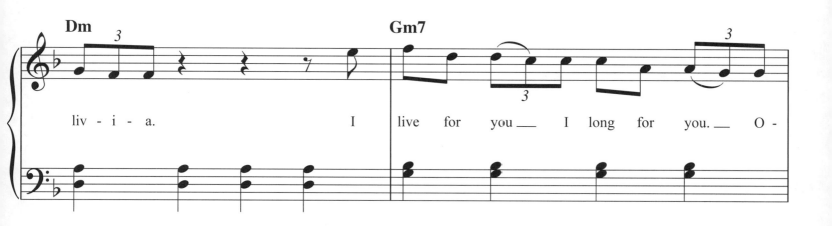

liv - i - a. I live for you __ I long for you. __ O -

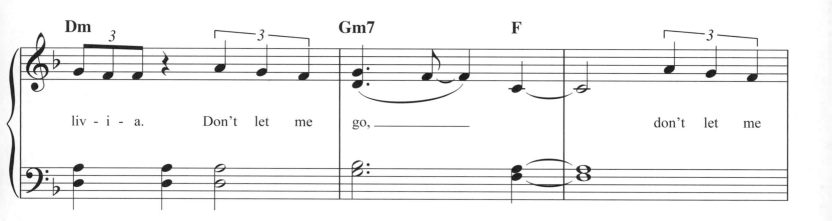

liv - i - a. Don't let me go, _____ don't let me

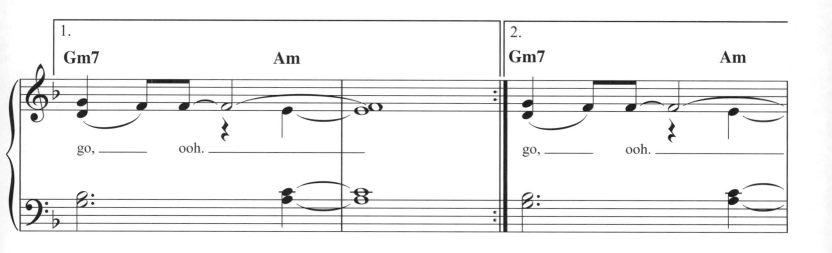

go, _____ ooh. _____   go, _____ ooh. _____

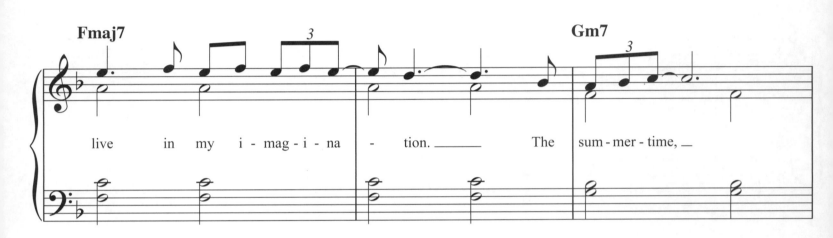

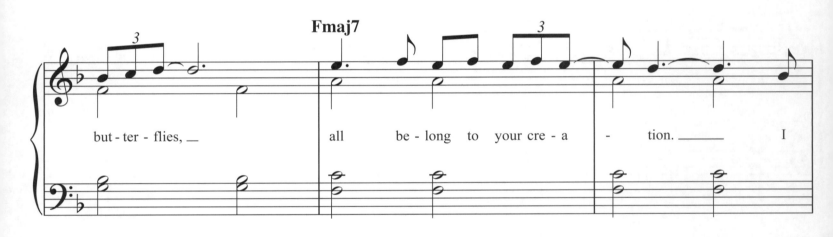

I live for you, I long for you, O - liv - i - a. I've been

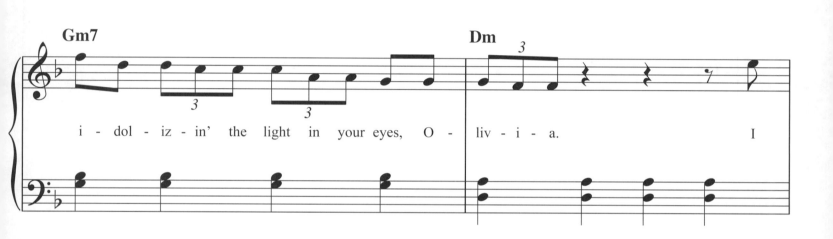

i - dol - iz - in' the light in your eyes, O - liv - i - a. I

live for you ___ I long for you. ___ O - liv - i - a. Don't let me

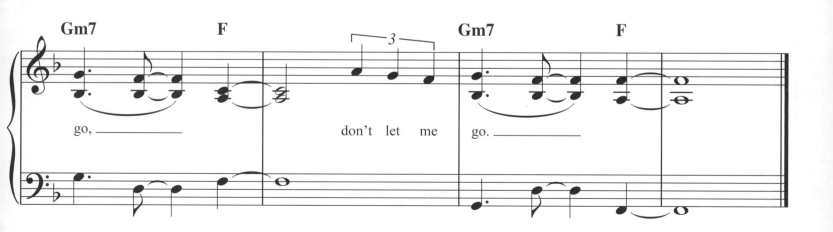

go, _____ don't let me go. _____

NEVER ENOUGH

Words and Music by NIALL HORAN,
JOHN HENRY RYAN, JULIAN BUNETTA
and JAMIE SCOTT

Moderately fast, with energy

Wan-na pull an all-night-er and get in-to some-thing we'll nev-er for-get.

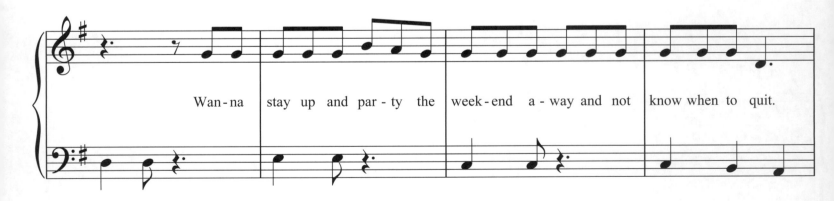

Wan-na stay up and par-ty the week-end a-way and not know when to quit.

Wan-na drive in the night till the end of the earth and go o-ver the edge.

Wan-na wake up with you and say, "Ba-by, let's do it all o-ver a-gain."

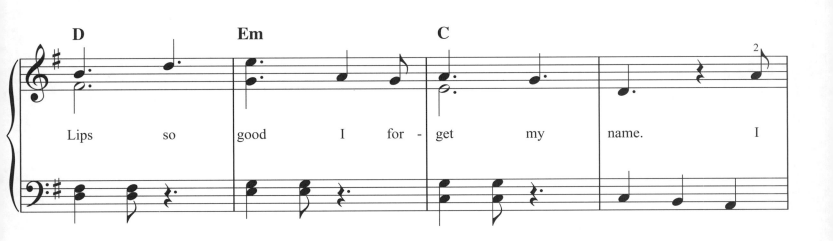

D   **Em**   **C**

Lips so good I for-get my name. I

D   **Em**   **C**

swear I could give you ev-'ry-thing. I

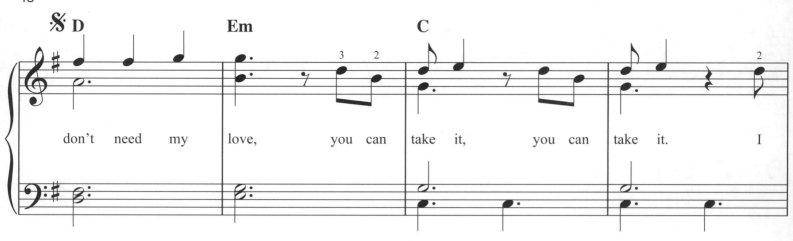

don't need my love, you can take it, you can take it. I

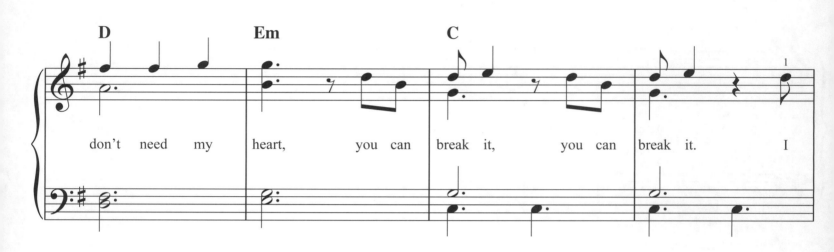

don't need my heart, you can break it, you can break it. I

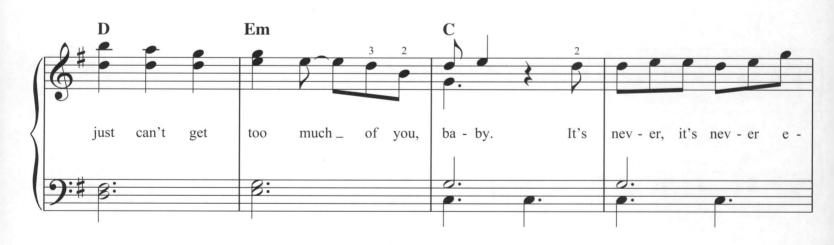

just can't get too much of you, ba - by. It's nev - er, it's nev - er e -

nough, nev - er e - nough, _____ it's nev - er e -

come on!

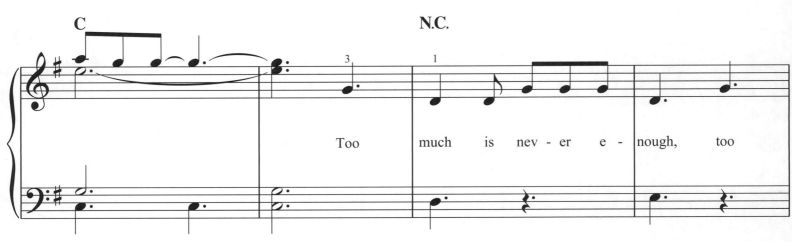

Too much is nev - er e - nough, too

much is nev - er e - nough, too much is nev - er e - nough, too

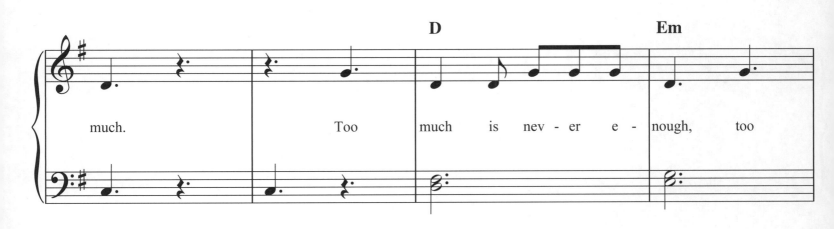

much. Too much is nev - er e - nough, too

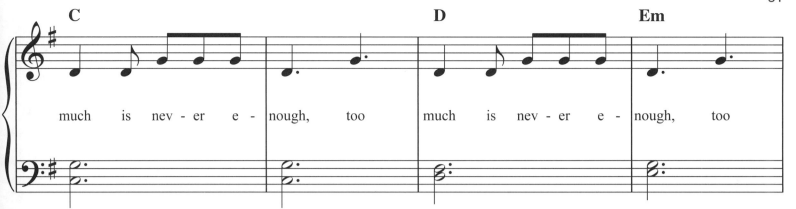

much is nev-er e-nough, too   much is nev-er e-nough, too

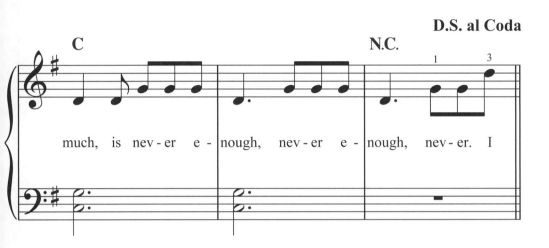

D.S. al Coda

N.C.

CODA

much, is nev-er e-nough, nev-er e-nough, nev-er. I

Come on!

Come on!

WHAT A FEELING

Words and Music by LIAM PAYNE,
LOUIS TOMLINSON, JAMIE SCOTT,
MIKE NEEDLE and DANIEL BRYER

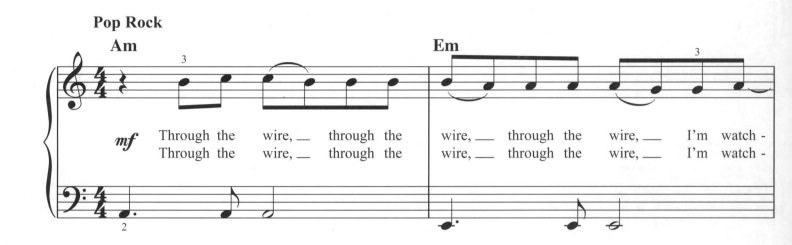

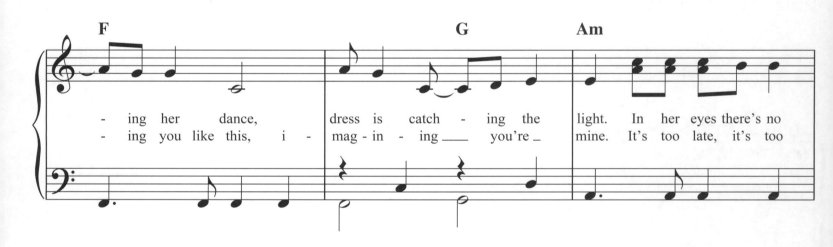

guise.
time? } With no ___ way out and a long ___ way down, ev - 'ry - bod - y

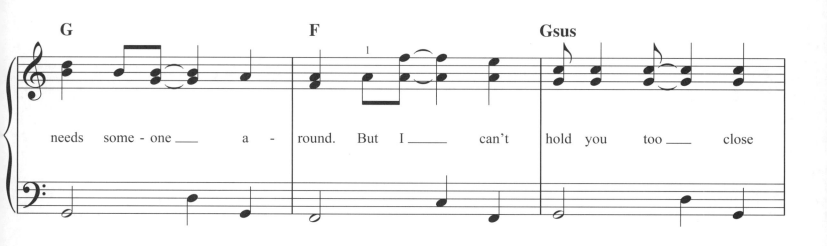

needs some - one ___ a - round. But I ___ can't hold you too ___ close

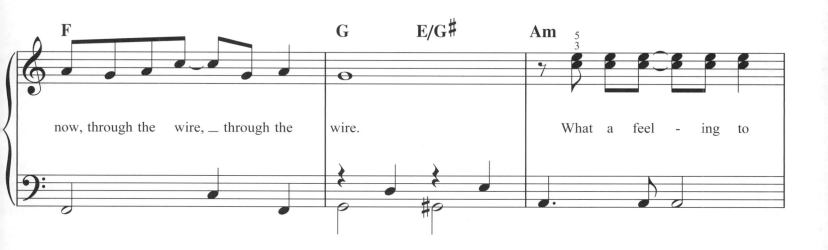

now, through the wire, ___ through the wire. What a feel - ing to

be right here ___ be - side you now, hold - ing you in ___ my

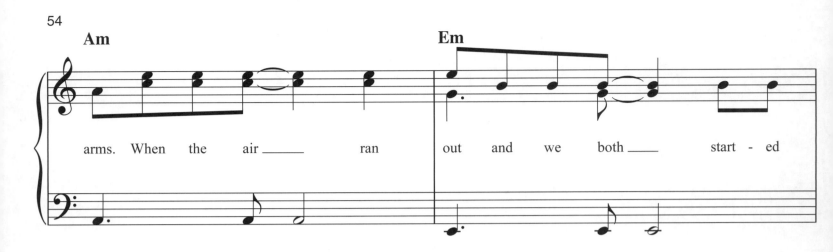

arms. When the air _____ ran out and we both _____ start - ed

run - ning wild, the sky fell down. _ But you've got stars _ there in

your eyes _____ and I've got some-thing miss - ing to - night. _

What a feel - ing to be a king _ be - side you, some - how, I

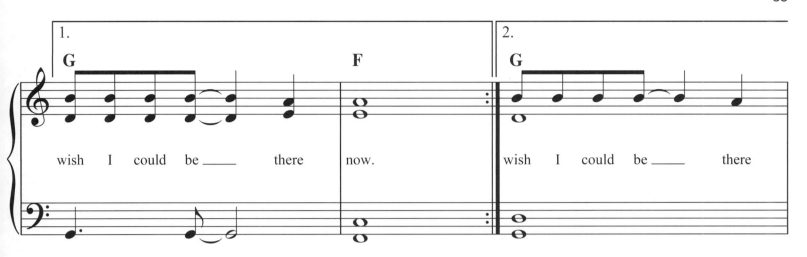

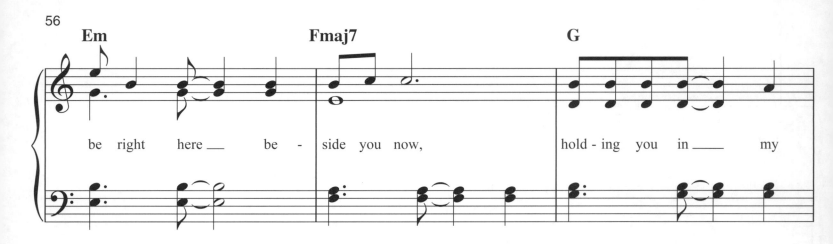

be right here ___ be - side you now, hold - ing you in ___ my

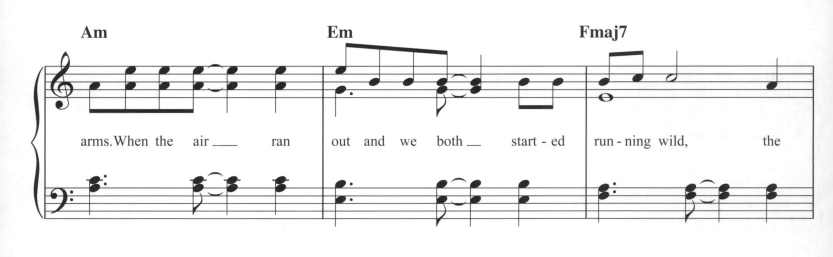

arms. When the air ___ ran out and we both ___ start - ed run - ning wild, the

sky fell down. _ But you've got stars ___ there in your eyes _____ and

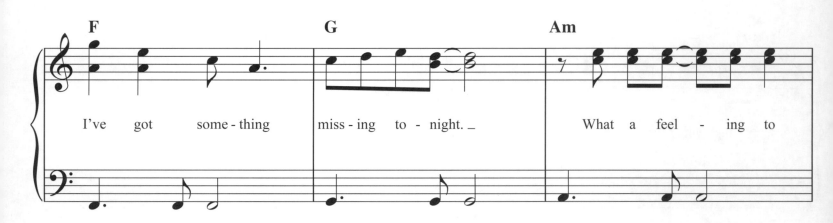

I've got some - thing miss - ing to - night. _ What a feel - ing to

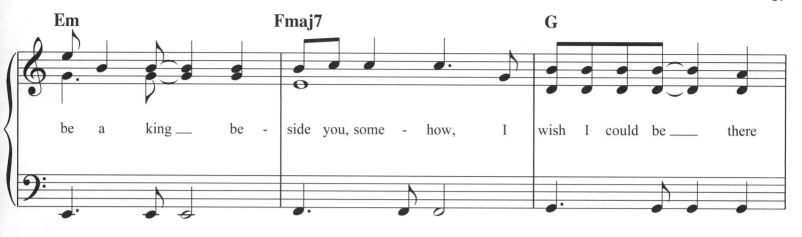

be a king ___ be - side you, some - how, I wish I could be ___ there

now. I

wish I could be ___ there now.

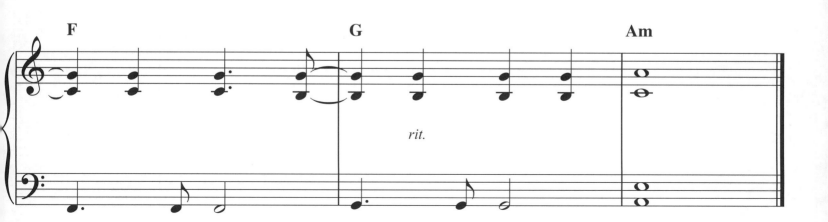

rit.

LOVE YOU GOODBYE

Words and Music by LOUIS TOMLINSON,
JULIAN BUNETTA and JACOB HINDLIN

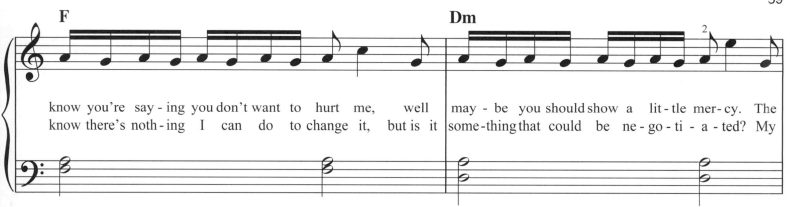

F ... **Dm**

know you're say-ing you don't want to hurt me, well | may-be you should show a lit-tle mer-cy. The
know there's noth-ing I can do to change it, but is it | some-thing that could be ne-go-ti-a-ted? My

F ... **G**

way you look I know you did-n't come to a-po-lo-|gize. } ... Hey. ____
heart's al-read-y break-ing, ba-by, go on, ___ twist the |knife. }

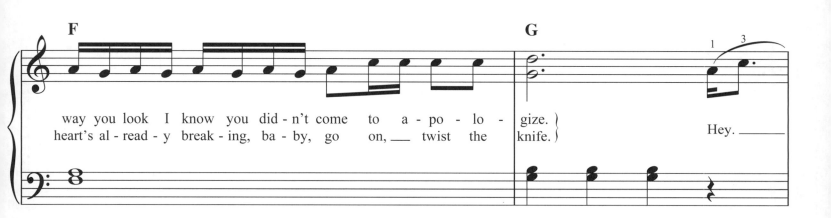

C **F** ... **G**

____ Oh, why you wear-ing that to walk out | of my life? ____ Hey. ____

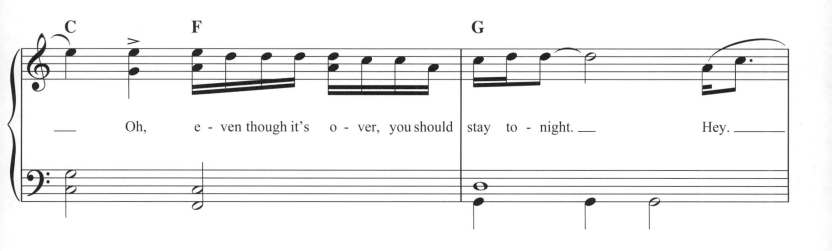

C **F** ... **G**

____ Oh, e-ven though it's o-ver, you should | stay to-night. ____ Hey. ____

If to-mor-row you can't be mine, won't you give it to me one last time?

Oh, ba-by, let me love you good - bye. _____ Un-for-

bye. Oh, ba-by, let me love you good -

bye. One more

taste of your lips __ just to bring __ me back to the plac - es we've been __ and the nights _ we've had. Be-cause

if this is it __ then at least __ we could end __ it right. __

Oh, why you wear - ing that to walk out of my life? __ Hey. __

__ Oh, e - ven though it's o - ver, you should stay to - night. __ Hey. __

I WANT TO WRITE YOU A SONG

Words and Music by JOHN HENRY RYAN,
JULIAN BUNETTA and AMMAR MALIK

I want to lend you my coat,
I want to build you a boat,

one that's as soft as your cheek.
one that's as strong as you are free,

So,
so

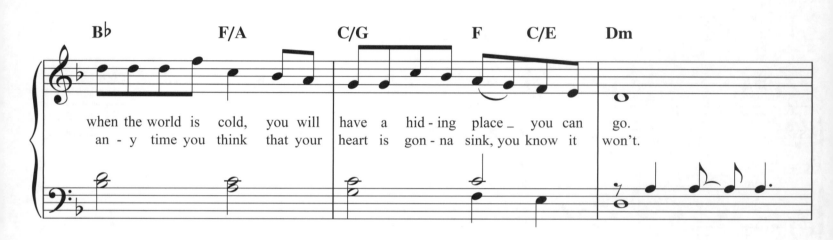

when the world is cold, you will have a hid - ing place _ you can go.
an - y time you think that your heart is gon - na sink, you know it won't.

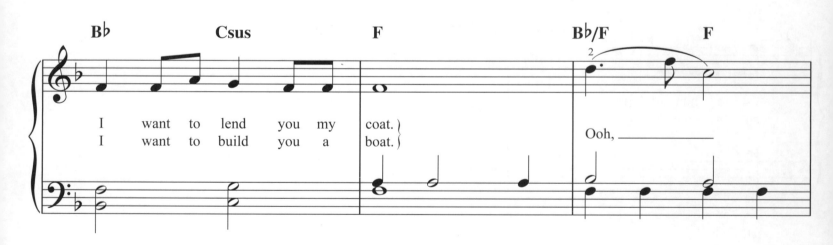

I want to lend you my coat.
I want to build you a boat.

Ooh, _____

ev - 'ry - thing I need I get from you. _____

HISTORY

Words and Music by LIAM PAYNE, LOUIS TOMLINSON,
JOHN HENRY RYAN, WAYNE ANTHONY HECTOR,
JULIAN BUNETTA and EDWARD DREWETT

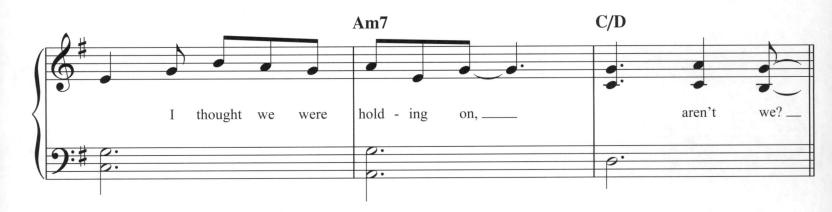

No, they don't teach you ___ this in school. ___
ru - mors, ___ all of the

fights, ___ Now my heart's break - ing and I
but we al - ways find a way to

don't know what to do. Thought we were go - ing strong, ___
make it out a - live. Thought we were go - ing strong, ___

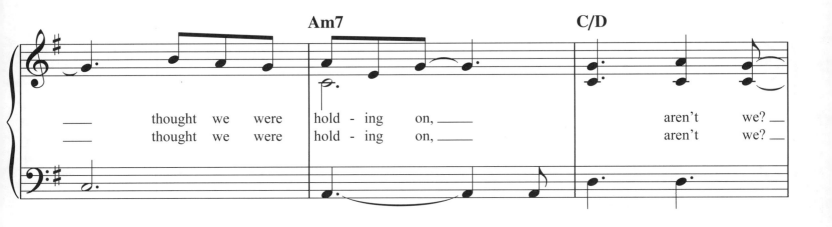

___ thought we were hold - ing on, ___ aren't we? ___
___ thought we were hold - ing on, ___ aren't we? ___

You and me got a

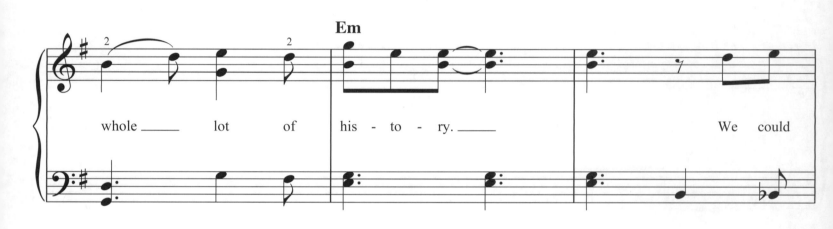

whole _____ lot of his - to - ry. _____ We could

be the great-est team _____ that the world has ev - er seen. _

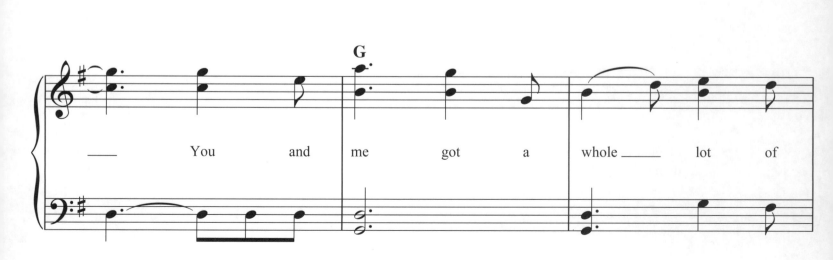

_____ You and me got a whole _____ lot of

his - to - ry. _____ So don't let it go, _____ we can

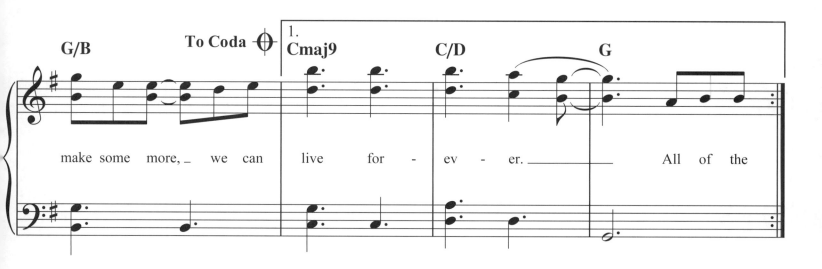

make some more,_ we can live for - ev - er. _____ All of the

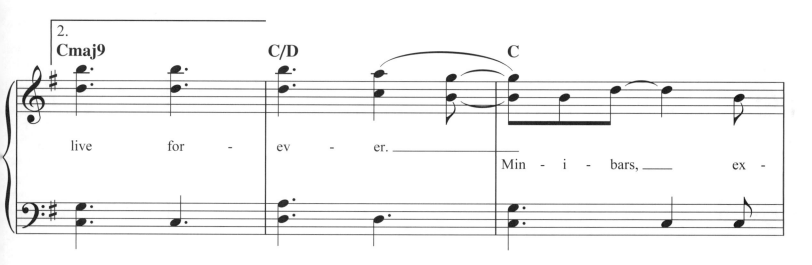

live for - ev - er. _____ Min - i - bars, _____ ex -

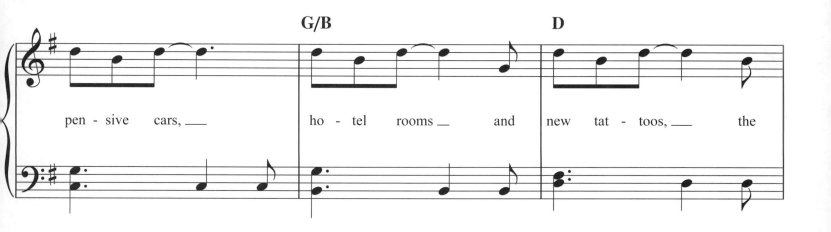

pen - sive cars, ___ ho - tel rooms ___ and new tat - toos, ___ the

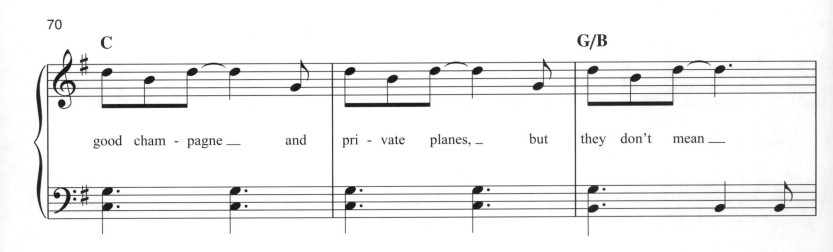

good cham - pagne ___ and pri - vate planes, __ but they don't mean ___

an - y - thing. __ 'Cause the truth is out, ___ I re - a - lize ___ that with -

out you here, ___ life is just a lie. ___ This is not the end, ___ this is

D.S. al Coda

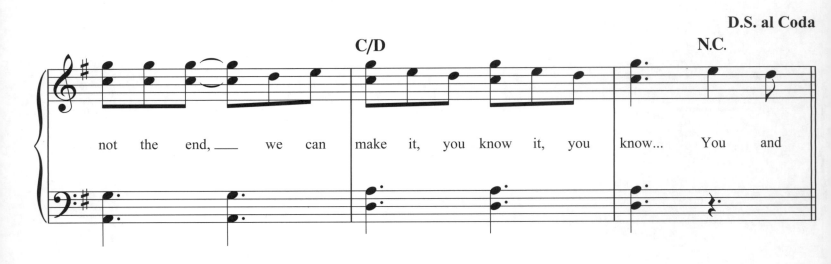

not the end, ___ we can make it, you know it, you know... You and